ATOMIC FIELD

BOOKS BY NICHOLAS CHRISTOPHER

POETRY
Atomic Field: Two Poems
The Creation of the Night Sky
5°
In the Year of the Comet
Desperate Characters: A Novella in Verse
A Short History of the Island of Butterflies
On Tour with Rita

FICTION
A Trip to the Stars
Veronica
The Soloist

NONFICTION
Somewhere in the Night: Film Noir & the American City

ANTHOLOGIES (AS EDITOR)
Walk on the Wild Side: Urban American Poetry since 1975
Under 35: The New Generation of American Poets

ATOMIC FIELD

Two Poems

Nicholas Christopher

Harcourt, Inc.

New York   San Diego   London

Requests for permission to make copies of any part of the work
should be mailed to the following address:
Permissions Department, Harcourt, Inc.,
6277 Sea Harbor Drive, Orlando, Florida 32887-6777.

Library of Congress Cataloging-in-Publication Data
Christopher, Nicholas.
Atomic Field: two poems / Nicholas Christopher.
p. cm.
ISBN 0-15-100553-2
I. Title.
PS3553.H754 A615 2000
811'.54—dc21   99-045142

Designed by Lydia D'moch
Text set in Spectrum
Printed in the United States of America
First edition
A C E G I J H F D B

ACKNOWLEDGMENTS

Some of the poems in this book first appeared in the following publications:

The New Yorker: "1972: 3" (Originally appeared as "The Séance, Paris 1972.")

The Paris Review: "1962: 20"

Tin House: "1972: 25, 27, 28, 29, 30"

Five Points: "1972: 1, 2, 4, 6, 9, 10, 13, 14, 23, 26"

Columbia Magazine: "1972: 15, 21, 37"

Washington Square Magazine: "1962: 3, 4, 5, 8, 12, 21"

for my brother, Paul

CONTENTS

ATOMIC FIELD

1962

1

Dry leaves fly across the empty street.
The sun is rising
and a dog is tearing laundry from the clothesline in the next yard.

In a vacant lot a boy my age—eleven this month—
is shooting tin cans off a barrel with a pellet gun.
When he thinks no one is watching,
he fires at the swallows on the telephone wire.
Finally he hits one, and stiffening with extended wings,
attempting flight, it spins to the sidewalk without a sound,
by which time the boy, looking over his shoulder,
lines up the cans again, as if nothing has happened.

3

I'm sitting at the window——a dead fly stuck
to the screen——in a white room
where the flaking paint drizzles from the ceiling
every time the man upstairs slams his door.
Or when the bikers go by in a phalanx, gunning their throttles.
Or when thunder rolls in over the river, preceded by lightning.
So the rubber plant on the table and the gardenia
that never flowers look as if they have been snowed on,
a fine silvery mountain snow,
unmeltable at the height of summer.

4

In the terrarium the turtles' shells are painted red-orange.
This is also the color of the dyed hair on the woman
in the wheelchair who smokes outside the laundry all day,
and the rust coating on the electrified fence at the lumberyard,
and the crayon I use to draw the house I'm in,
which is really gray.

5

A bicycle without wheels upended in the sun.
An electric saw chewing through plywood.
Beside the smashed-up car in front
of the house with the collapsed roof
a man is filling a yellow pail with shards of glass,
blood speckling his shirt
and all the fingers missing on his left hand
from an accident long ago.

6

The black-and-white television in this room
comes on whenever you enter,
immediately rendering you gray—
a shade slipping through the spectral twilight.
When you leave the room,
its sad heavy furniture, see-through curtains, threadbare carpet,
the television goes off.
Only once did it stay on,
and that was for someone who died the following week
and for years afterward appeared on the screen sporadically,
an extra in old movies,
a bystander in breaking news stories,
someone forever at the fringes of a milling crowd.

7

A girl is dyeing her bathing suit blue in a tub of hot water.
Her dog named Mambo is watching her.
The suit was originally white.
Mambo is white, with black spots on his head.
The girl says her mother, the widow, does the mambo
in their living room on Friday nights.
Sometimes with a man.
The next time I see the girl she tells me
that when she wore the bathing suit to the beach,
all the dye came out in the blue water.
Then she lifts her skirt to show me,
and her suit is white again, all right,
above her thin, suntanned legs.

8

On the back porch after an afternoon of driving rain
that swept the robins' nest
from the upper reaches of the pin oak,
I'm trying to play solitaire with a pinochle deck.
From a book I bought for a dime I have taught myself
how to play double-solitaire,
a game which over the course of the year
I will win only once (without cheating).

A pile of comic books, alphabetically and chronologically arranged:
Aquaman
Batman
Green Lantern
and, of course, *Superman,*
who by squeezing it in his fist
can convert a chunk of coal
into a diamond,
but today finds himself chained and manacled
in a cage of green kryptonite
on a meteor streaking through space,
the thick chains also hammered of kryptonite,
the meteor kryptonite too.
So he feels like all the rest of us for a few minutes—
except that he gets to escape.

10

After buying jawbreakers, red hots, and five packs of baseball cards,
I'm browsing at the candy store.
A discarded cigar is burning on the lip of the curb.
A pigeon circles it, bobbing.
It's rush hour and people are streaming in crosscurrents
past the pay phones, the kiosks,
the vending machines in the arcade.
I pick up an automotive magazine
filled with glossy photos of futuristic models:
cars that run on batteries or power cells,
electric cars and atomic cars,
and best of all, a car that will travel
five hundred miles on ten gallons of water.
The *Hydromobile,* it's called,
and according to the caption
it will be coming off the assembly line
in the year 2162,
two hundred years from now.
In an illustration beside the photo
a man in a kind of space suit,
with his wife and children also in space suits,
is standing in his driveway
filling the car's fuel tank with a garden hose.
His split-level house with the brick chimney
doesn't look very futuristic.
Meanwhile, in front of the candy store,
an old man picks up the burning cigar stub
and walks away smoking it.

II

The rain clouds bring no rain.
Dust-colored, they settle over the river.
A biplane buzzes through them like a mosquito.
It looks like a crop duster, or one of those planes
that seeds clouds with dry ice.
Following a figure eight, trailing a pennant—
NOW AT THE RIALTO—
it skywrites the titles of today's double feature:
EXPERIMENT IN TERROR & *UNDERWORLD U.S.A.*
I go to the Rialto and for a dollar
get admission, a bag of popcorn, and a 7-Up.
In the first movie, the villain kidnaps a girl,
takes off her dress, and locks her in a storage vault;
later, he's shot by the police
on a baseball diamond in San Francisco.
Between features, in a Civil Defense short,
the ghosts of children who died in an atomic war
explain why they didn't go to the nearest fallout shelter.
In the second movie, the hero,
after witnessing his father's gangland murder,
becomes a gangland murderer himself
until one day he too is gunned down.
By the time I leave the theater,
night has fallen and it's raining finally,
lights running like paint on the gleaming streets
and strangers everywhere—a world
of them—averting their eyes.

12

A four-story building.
Gray brick with brown trim.
A brown door lighted by a yellow bulb that repels insects.
Eight identical apartments.
Flowerpots in some of the windows.
A fire escape which I climb
to the roof at night.
Reclining on the tar paper
beneath a jumble of television antennae,
I watch the jets with flashing pinpoint lights
arc in and out of the airport,
always along the same three routes.
Later I concentrate on the stars,
which constantly change position
while appearing never to move.

13

The old woman upstairs with the canary that doesn't sing
bleaches her shell collection once a year
in her claw-foot tub
while listening to the records she and her husband
used to play at the beach cottage they rented
every summer for thirty years, until he died.
Those records all have the same choppy, unceasing hiss
in the background, like the sea
when we live right beside it
and can no longer hear it apart from everything else.

14

There is always someone on crutches in this luncheonette.
Or so it seems.
A former GI.
A bus driver who was hit by a truck.
A nurse who never recovered from polio.
And behind the counter, the bald man
with the hook for a hand,
who can twirl his moustache with it.

15

Snow slants through the trees in the park.
The clouds are sinking, heavy as iron.
In here, by the sputtering radiator,
there are rows of fish under glass,
on beds of crushed ice,
with lemon slices in their gills.
Silver-black, pink, pale blue,
all of them lying on their sides, one-eyed—
the one eye vaporous as Venus,
but frozen fast, like the planet
if it ever spun to a stop.

16

A dead branch ticks like a clock against the attic window.
Across the street, the butcher, heavyset with a crew cut,
runs a flag up the pole in his yard.
Two houses down, the retired dentist on clear nights
tilts a telescope out his fourth-floor window
to observe the stars and planets.
I have also seen him spy on the butcher's wife
when she sunbathes on her roof.
Sometimes I encounter him at the candy store,
stroking his beard and buying magazines
like *Astronomy* and *Starwatch,*
and, from another rack, *Heavenly Bodies,*
that features a girl on the cover provocatively posed,
currently in one of the polka-dot bikinis
which are the rage all summer.
Night and day on the radio they play a song
that celebrates the yellow polka-dot variety.
The butcher's wife, getting her mail,
can be glimpsed in her bikini,
polka-dotted not in yellow
but red, white, and blue.

17

It's morning again.
The wind is raw.
Smoke is seeping through the treetops
where the foliage is thickest, greenest.
The hard chatter of the birds is ebbing.
The street cleaner, the milkman, the postman,
they're all coming, one by one, in uniform,
like the stragglers at the end of a parade that passed long ago,
or the first scouts in an army that will never arrive.

On the peaked roof of the funeral parlor
the rooster on the weathervane
is so rusted it cannot spin.
Alighting on the rooster, a crow surveys the blue street.
He may live to be seventy—
longer than most of the people
who will be laid out below in satin-lined caskets.
On the sidewalk a tired violinist improvises,
and the flower girl, who might have stepped
from the chapel's stained glass window,
is running her errands:
valerian from the apothecary, to help her sleep;
sesame oil, for sautéing shrimp with the heads on,
and a silver hammer to nail up the cheap print
of the Last Supper in the projection booth
of the movie house where she works nights.
In the print, Judas Iscariot raises his goblet,
spilling some drops onto his hands and feet
where they bead, like blood.
On the road to suicide, he is already
bent out of shape—like so many people—
by repeated blows he has not yet received.

19

In the time it takes the cold sunlight
to slide across the windblown street,
how many people have been born
and how many have died
around the world,
in this city,
within a mile of this house,
where such information is not always welcome.

20

At the bus stop a blind man sells colored pencils.
Ballpoint pens, too, at Thanksgiving and Christmas.
Ten cents for a pencil, two bits for a pen.
Around the corner, a boy from the orphanage
gives a bookmark to anyone who drops money into his box—
no matter if it's a nickel or a dollar.
A different boy every day, rotating by the month.
There are that many boys at the orphanage, I am told,
and I am grateful not to be one and fearful that I could be—
these boys in their coarse blue suits and thick-soled black shoes,
faces alternately fierce and frightened
and in their eyes the sad lights of distant ports
faintly flickering as they repeat the same refrain:
Alms for Saint Gregory,
the name of their orphanage,
the patron saint of shipwrecked sailors,
of lost travelers.

21

I wander onto a flagstone path
near my house
that I will never find again,
where sunlight casts jagged
shadows through the pines,
making the end of the path
seem like a place I can never reach;
and even when I do, it feels
like another place altogether—
not the zone of shadows and wind I expect,
but a gentle slope giving onto
a wide lawn unbrokenly lit.

22

At P.S. 28:
girls with budding breasts in Girl Scout uniforms;
classmates arm wrestling for quarters;
teachers (all women) smoking and applying makeup in their
    lounge;
a principal who sprinkles her speeches with Latin words;
a janitor with a red toupee
and a one-armed gym coach.
This is the place where I learn to read;
to give and take a punch in the playground;
to lie when absolutely necessary;
to multiply and divide;
to switch hit a baseball;
to recite a poem by heart before an audience.
The poem is "Trees" by Joyce Kilmer
(the only work of his I will ever encounter)
and with it I conclude the tree-planting ceremony
in honor of a student who died of cancer.
Why I am chosen to play this role I don't know.
But that night I write my own version of the poem—
which I show no one—only to discover
with astonishment and secret delight
that I prefer it to the original.

On television
the alternate world
of current events—
like a fantasy—
is always available,
its signposts ever-shifting:
Cuba and Berlin
NATO and SEATO
Mobutu and Lumumba
U-2
A-OK
and all the way with JFK;
Tito Nasser Nehru
Formosa and Laos
and barely audible behind the din,
across the sea of static
where the ghost ships sail,
Vietnam

Six doors down, a beautiful young woman
with golden hair lives alone in a yellow house.
She always dresses in yellow and gold
and wears heels, gloves, and amber glasses year round.
I don't know her name.
Working nights, coming home at dawn,
she is the subject of endless unflattering
speculation among the neighbors.
I think she might be a magician's assistant,
or one of the Rockettes.
She drives a two-tone Triumph—mustard & ochre—
touching the dashboard lighter to the cigarette
between her lips whenever she speeds around the corner.
Only after she isn't seen for a week
do we discover that she was a night court stenographer
who disappeared without a trace one morning.
Eventually her house is sold.
The new owner paints it white,
but to his surprise finds that no matter
what color tulips and roses he plants in the garden,
they always come up yellow, as do
the cherry tomatoes on their tangled vines.
And that after a solitary yellow canary
builds a nest in the one tree in the yard,
the apples sprouting on its branches shine gold—
a marvel, seeing that it isn't an apple tree at all.

25

In my most recurring nightmare
a wolf with a broken leg is trapped
with me in a freight elevator.
We're plunging down a shaftway flashing with green lights.
The wolf is snarling.
I keep circling away from him,
but he's cutting off the angle on me.
Closing in.
His leg is caked with blood.
His rolling eyes are white.
Finally we're falling so fast I can barely breathe
and the wolf rises up on his one good leg,
bows, and pulls from his throat
first my best friend
and then my friend's dog,
and though they're both dead
the dog is barking
and my friend is shouting at me,
"Jump—jump!"
But there's nowhere to jump from,
and nothing to jump to.

26

At the bend, weeping willows overhang the tracks.
The trains fly by, silver and black:
northward on the hour, southward on the half hour.
A swan is sleeping on the lake,
his neck and head like a question mark against the darkness.
But the night belongs to the insects:
fireflies like electrons, clouds of gnats,
dragonflies streaming colors,
and moths that zigzag frantically
in search of lights—
house lights, street lights, flashlights,
even the lights of an oncoming train.

27

Successive snowstorms have lined the streets
with bands of ice, like sedimentary stone.
While his wife is being fitted for fur-lined boots,
the undertaker is holding forth in the shoe store
about the fine points of burial in frozen ground,
edifying the clerk, who's looking up the wife's skirt.
The undertaker has the tidiest, tightest garden on our street,
maintained by moonlighting workmen from the cemetery.
He himself never puts a spade to earth at home.
He spends his free time in the garage,
regularly steaming clean the components of his car engine,
then reassembling it—the V-8 from a 1950 Cadillac sedan,
black as coal, that runs so quietly
you can't hear it, even on the stillest night.

With a shard of ice I scratch my name
on the surface of the frozen lake:
as ice cuts into ice, can a diamond
 (which leaves its mark on all things)
scratch another diamond?
And if so, is it the superior—more valuable—
diamond that prevails, or the dime-a-dozen variety?
No such question arises with ice,
which any way you cut it, is H_2O;
my name's engraved on it,
and though it may be covered by snow
and worn down by wind,
will remain so until the lake thaws,
returning to that blackness with which I was one
before I ever had a name.

In the complexities of the figured carpet
a red key is concealed
among grapes, plums, and pomegranates.
Coming in from the snow,
I pick up the key, make my way
down the rickety stairs,
and unlock the door to the cellar,
where a man is operating a winepress by candlelight.
His face is flushed and he wears a red vest.
He's propped a color print of Bacchus
on one of the casks: a curly-haired young man
in a tunic who's arcing a stream of wine
into his mouth from a leather canteen.
A crescent of stars is tattooed on his forehead.
His eyes, rolling back, reflect the moon,
and his followers, draped in animal skins,
reel in his wake, the crushed grapes
bleeding through their fingers
just like the ones this man in the cellar
is holding up to me with a cold smile.

30

In my bed, breathing stale air, I see an army crossing
deserts and frozen wastes, scaling mountains,
fording turbulent rivers, losing its soldiers to attrition,
so that the opposing army, awaiting them on a misty battlefield
finally disperses, first planting a blank flag on which each of us
can draw his insignia: mine a pair of eyes gazing into a sky
where the bruised clouds will one day gather finally,
dramatically, though like everyone else,
I will somehow miss seeing them, even as thousands of men die
and thousands more—pitched toward death—are born.

Our street is shaped like a boomerang,
and everyone who lives on it knows
that whatever you do in this life comes back—
an hour, or ten years, later—
to torment you, or maybe knock your head off.
Try to get away and you'll end up right where you started.
In the bowling alley, the pins fly
off the face of the earth with a thunderous crash.
In the sky, the summer storm approaches like a drumroll.
And all the while the girls in their dresses cut from the darkness
line up to board the crosstown bus,
which will follow its elliptical route
from one end of town to the other—
and back again.

32

Rooftops
of television antennae tortuously twisted
to pick up distant signals
and clotheslines flapping with the primary colors
and the occasional pigeon coop,
and at the very end of the street
the greenhouse where the numismatist
when he is not in his tiny shop
where every cabinet and drawer is always kept locked
cultivates hydroponic tomatoes from Egypt
and orchids from Java.
He is also an amateur painter.
Beneath billowing clouds he paints his self-portrait:
a man in a white jacket
with a tomato in one hand
and a Flemish guilder in the other,
poised between his thumb and forefinger,
flashing like the sun.

At least three women on the street
have bleached and combed their hair in the billowing style
she made famous
and two of them even wear hot pink from head to toe
through the August heat wave
when the newspapers are filled with photographs of her
and her surprisingly unassuming cottage,
its short cement driveway
lined with hydrangea bushes, and oleanders
whose sap is poisonous as snake venom,
down which they carried her body,
so small suddenly in the black rubber bag,
to an ambulance where the driver
sat frozen in bright sunlight.
MARILYN the headlines blare day after day,
who never again will blow a kiss
laughing from an open window,
never with a careless gesture throw off
the blanket of white roses that covers her now.

There is the woman who like Leonardo buys caged birds
in order to set them free.
And her husband who prefers sitting on their front porch
for hours killing flies with a flyswatter.
He works as an electrician at the opera house.
But the only music I ever hear from their living room,
through the green chintz curtains,
are her LPs of show tunes:
Gypsy, South Pacific, West Side Story,
over and over again....
One day she brings home a caged bird,
a kind of blackbird with red-tipped wings that sings,
which she actually keeps.
Within a week it dies,
and the husband buries it in their garden,
and for a long time I hear no music from that house.

The flesh the flesh-eating plants eat
turns out to be houseflies and ants
which the librarian daily introduces
through sliding panels in the terraria
that sit beneath a tall window in the lobby
where the motes of dust perpetually spin:
the Cobra Plant, the Sundew, the Yellow Pitcher,
and of course the Venus Flytrap *(Dionaea muscipula)*
whose flowers themselves are fleshlike, waxy.
This is a common characteristic among the members
of the *Droseraceae* family,
which also are noted for
their tufts of hair and bloodlike sap.
A neatly typed sign on the wall
adds that there are larger varieties
in South America capable of entrapping
birds and rodents, and in Malaysia
a colony of the *Nepenthes* family
which is rumored to thrive on wild goats
and the occasional human being,
and that for obvious reasons
none of these plants will be exhibited any time soon.
In front of the library
the hot dog vendor smears mustard, relish, and onions
on his twenty-five-cent special
which it is pleasant to eat slowly,
sitting in the sun on the granite steps
and watching the cars go by.

Under the microscope the chains of cells
in their red clouds are multiplying,
subdividing, mutating, flying apart—
a universe in miniature,
which is called a microcosm.
Billions of them in our bloodstreams.
Billions of us on earth.
Worlds unto ourselves someone has written
on the flyleaf of a hymn book
I find on a park bench in the rain.
Beyond the grain of sand
or particle of dust,
invisible to the naked eye,
is the realm of the microscopic
and (as of 1912) the submicroscopic,
which is called *microcosmos.*
In the end, thousands—no, hundreds—
of years from now,
we'll all be living there.

37

On the lawn of the house that burned down,
there is a dollhouse which also burned.
A doll hangs from an upstairs window
with scorched hair and melted hands.
As for the little girl who owned the dollhouse,
her parents, their terrier, and a Panamanian songbird,
no trace has yet been found by the firemen
knee-deep in rubble, their faces smeared
with ashes in the red light of dawn.

On the 9th of October I am told to say my prayers.
On television entire congregations in cathedrals
are shown to be on their knees, clutching candles and praying.
In Cuba, ninety miles from Florida,
nuclear missiles are directed at American cities,
first and foremost New York
where I too light a candle and go on my knees
beside my bed for only the second time in my life to pray
that I will reach my twelfth birthday, in February,
and that the president will see his way through the darkness
to a place where none of us will have to die.
The first time I prayed like this was on the night
last year when my grandfather was dying.
And he died soon afterward.
(The next time will be a year from now,
on the day the president is shot,
and he too will die soon afterward.)
But tonight I fall asleep reviewing the zigzag route
I will follow to the nearest fallout shelter,
at the Masonic lodge,
and the posture I will assume—
knees tucked up, head buried in my arms—
when a wall of fire topples the city like a toy,
only to wake to the news that the crisis has ended,
the missiles are being shipped back to Russia.
We're safe again.

39

A kite gold and round as the sun
spins down from the clouds,
growing larger by the second,
trailing a burning string.
The farther it falls, the hotter everything gets:
flowers wilt, trees shed their leaves,
glasses of water boil.
Finally, the heat is unbearable,
and as my shoes sink into the asphalt
in a cloud of smoke, I'm thinking
maybe it's the sun after all
when suddenly a boy in a red shirt,
his hair dancing like a flame,
runs around the corner, pointing to the sky,
and shouts that he's lost his kite.

When my friend casts his line by moonlight,
the fish stream to it.
Night fishing is his specialty.
Making his way downstream by zigzagging
over the many footbridges that span the still pools
where the trout hover, quicker than shadows.
Returning home just before dawn
with his basket full of fish
and sometimes too the pockets of his jeans
and the even deeper pockets of his worn corduroy jacket
with the bloodstains on the sleeves
and the smell so strong
that I pick it up long before I see or hear him
down the street with his rod over his shoulder
when he comes to dig for worms
under the pachysandra in my yard.
The fish trust that smell, he tells me,
that's why they come to me.

In pointy shoes that lace up the sides—twist shoes—
and pancho shirts that don't tuck in
people are doing the twist.
Round and round and up and down…
That's Chubby Checker in his signature black suit
and patent leather shoes
that lace up the sides
twisting on the Ed Sullivan Show.
And Joey Dee and the Starlighters at a row of mikes
under pink spotlights
at the Peppermint Lounge
way over on the West Side
where the line of people waiting to get in,
their coats and hats white with snow,
stretches for four blocks.
And the name of the dance is the "Peppermint Twist"…
On the radio you can hear the twist night and day.
At the school dance no other dance is danced.
Everybody's doing it,
come on, baby, and do the twist.
In the auditorium one day, drifting off collectively into a golden haze,
we're told the times are complex by a visiting psychologist.
That no point is reached by way of a straight line.
And no one can insist anymore that he alone knows
right from wrong, and then enforce that knowledge.
Not with the specter of the mushroom cloud hovering.
I notice that even the psychologist is wearing twist shoes.
Round and round and up and down…

The tallest pines are swaying, and snow has buried the stone walls.
What appears to be a black bird on a half-toppled post
is a girl's sweater, neatly draped, with the sleeves tied in a bow.
Through the arbor gate enormous icicles are suspended
from the barn's gutter, orange at their centers
with a fire that cannot melt them.
Meanwhile, there is no sign of the girl who removed her sweater,
not a single footstep in the snow—near that post,
through the arbor, in or out of the woods.
How cold she must be, I'm thinking, wherever she is.

43

In a packed movie house on Christmas Day
I'm watching a girl in a loincloth,
longhaired with honey-colored skin,
emerge from the surf with a knife in her teeth.
A man is crossing two oceans to sleep with her.
Connoisseur of fast cars, crack shot,
he is a man of strong appetites and silence,
with an unshakable faith in the finality of death.
A spy.
Equipped with eyeglasses that penetrate the night
and cuff links packed with nitro,
he can transform his watch into a radar screen
with a flick of the wrist.
Backdropped by flames, wreckage, dying men,
with the glowing darkness of the Cold War,
he is the man of illusion who has no illusions,
whose adversary—a mad scientist
extravagant as Caligula—goes by the name of No.

In a house outlined by Christmas lights,
where wreaths hang in the windows
and plastic reindeer are spotlighted on the lawn,
girls in long nightgowns, like ghosts,
stand before mirrors and comb out their hair,
hundreds of brushstrokes into the night.
I'm a houseguest, sitting by the fire,
when one of them lets me in on her recurring dream:
an alpine plateau dotted with crosses,
beneath glass peaks,
where she's a climber caught in an avalanche.
And every time I dream it, she says,
another hair on my head turns white.

45

A girl in white is rowing across the lake,
skirting the waterfall,
drifting into the green vapors
where the reeds stir
and the clouds blow to sea.
This is the day on which she will disappear for all time.
A mile up, snow geese pass in formation.
Deep in the woods, a wolf is howling.
At the bottom of the lake the flashing moon spins among the
    weeds.
That girl's hair flares visibly for miles,
its fire freezing into the tenuous threads,
the glassy tendrils, at the center of a pink gem—
cold when the sun rises,
cold when the sun sets.

1972

1

On New Year's Eve,
having dropped five hundred mikes of acid at ten-thirty
in order to feel the first rushes at midnight,
we turn the stereo up,
place the speakers in the window facing outward,
and recline on the Indian carpet
with the burgundy and orange renderings of Vishnu and Lakshmi
locked in coitus,
the sun blazing on his forehead,
the moon on hers.
And locked together ourselves,
the carpet now streaming thousands of colors
into an arc that spans the room,
a rainbow of electrical impulses
beneath which we are protected forever
from the forces of the night,
the darkness pressing into this building
at the center of the city,
we suddenly hear beating wings fast approaching
and realize it is Vayu, the god of wind,
ruler of the fallen realms,
who is streaking across the sea,
beneath blue clouds,
to carry off everyone but us.
For at dawn, it's true, we're still here,
shivering on the floor of this empty room
where the steam pipes knock and hiss
but produce no heat.

2

Chain-smoking with one hand on the steering wheel,
gazing into a sky where all the planets and their moons are visible,
listening to a band of drummers on the radio through waves of
   static,
I keep the speedometer steady at 75 from New York to Boston.
Your buckskin jacket with the fringes is open,
your silk shirt unbuttoned to the waist
and the map light glowing on your bare breasts
as you roll a joint with one hand,
stroke my cheek with the other,
your eyes washed-out as the winter sea
gazing through the forest of bare trees
to the darkness that is colder than the cold.

3

A room illuminated by the rays of black crystals
arranged in a perfect circle on the lacquered table.
Beside them, a checkered cloth with talismans
we can move from square to square
while behind the curtain an invisible woman,
plucking a single note on a Japanese harp,
divines the future.
In the corner, the wick of a red candle flames to life.
A clock strikes six o'clock.
And none of us sitting around this table—
itself a revolving circle within the square room—
know if it's morning or evening.
To which someone remarks, Why should it matter?
And all the while the moon is rising full
between the thin buildings,
its mountains and seas icily clear,
easily mapped—unlike the landscapes
we're roaming in our heads,
the vast, inked-in expanses
where everything is possible and nothing changes.

4

In the waiting room a woman
in a Salvation Army coat and scuffed boots
who has accompanied her sister
is sipping weak coffee from a Styrofoam cup
and staring down a dark linoleum corridor
when she tells me she read somewhere
that in a single second 1.2 million people
around the world arrive and depart
in railroad terminals and airports,
at bus stops, taxi queues, and ferry slips.
"Everything is in motion and every place is a station," she adds,
"even this place."
Neither of us says another word
before the man who was once a doctor
in his pale green gown and horn-rimmed glasses
comes through the door expressionless
and nods to me that it's over with the woman
I accompanied there in the predawn, who was,
and is no longer, two months pregnant by my friend.
He is in jail for hurling blood
onto the windows of the recruiting center
to protest the war.
And now his girlfriend and the doctor have broken
the law, with me a silent witness,
an accomplice, but not yet
a criminal myself as far as I know.

5

On my twenty-first birthday I find myself
at the edge of the desert
with a map of the stars—
not the ones in the sky overhead,
but in galaxies where even now time is just beginning.
Stars we will never see in our own lifetimes:
the ones that light up behind the eyes
of the baby about to be born
and the man who takes his dying breath.

6

Occasionally a passerby will tramp past the basement window,
only his slush-covered boots visible from the disordered room
where she moves back and forth from the sink to the stove,
one strap of her red slip down around her elbow
and her red hair wild, stirring a pot,
preparing a meal for the bearded man naked
under a quilt dotted with cigarette burns
on a sofa with no legs, Daffy Duck on the portable
television inches from his sleeping face, talking
his way out of a jam with a scowling bulldog-headed policeman,
and nailed to the wall over the mattress in the corner
a technicolor poster of a windswept shipwrecked couple,
beautiful in their rags, in a movie called *Island of the Doomed.*

7

When she comes off her shift at the VA hospital
where she tends the recent arrivals from Vietnam,
the amputees and paraplegics
and the shell-shocked boys,
some of them younger than me,
who often wake, she tells me,
feeling pain in their missing limbs,
we rendezvous near the boathouse,
watching the scullers fly by,
or at the old cemetery
on a cement bench
hidden among the hawthorn bushes.
She's still in uniform,
white stockings, shoes, and the dress
that I unbutton just far enough
to slip my hand in over her breasts
when we start to kiss
there in the sun,
and she always touches
my legs and my arms
one by one before embracing me fully
as the wind picks up off the river
and carries the scents of the flowers
that grow wild on its banks.

8

From the full moon where volcanoes once erupted,
across a quarter million icy miles,
snow is spinning down,
dry as lunar ash,
filling the canyons of the city,
bringing all activity, high and low, to a standstill.
Even those of us already static or solipsistic
stop whatever it is
we're doing in our heads.
And according to the man
in the thin coat and dark glasses
shivering at the corner,
ringing his bell,
all's right with the world.

9

The pulse I feel behind my knees,
in my groin,
at the base of my skull
is echoed in the music you're playing,
broadcast from other galaxies
and picked up by radio telescopes.
Those stars are so cold and faraway
and you're so close and warm,
opening your arms,
your mouth,
and in the next breath your legs
under this rough woolen blanket
with the mazelike pattern—
a map of the Apache spirit world—
on the cabin's pine floor.
One day you'll be as faraway
as those stars—
no, farther—
and sending back no music.

We're in a theater.
Layers of smoke rising.
Strobe lights.
Screeching static.
A midget dressed like Sherlock Holmes,
puffing a calabash, is leading a fat man on a leash.
A topless girl has painted bull's-eyes on her breasts.
No, someone says, that's a Hindu symbol for death-in-life—
the sacred place at the center of all circles.
From the balcony some bikers are pouring
apricot brandy into the orchestra seats.
Onstage the light is bloodred, pooling in the corners.
A spider tattooed on his face,
the drummer lays down a beat,
the bass follows, then the guitars
like jet engines revving up
inside the monolithic speakers.
"I'm at Stonehenge," the girl with the bull's-eyes
says to no one in particular,
who replies that, hey, that's cool, but he's in Tunis,
where it's midnight, worshipping Isis
as she sheds moonlit tears in her black temple.
Suddenly a gunshot rings out in the balcony,
the fat man escapes his leash
and girls rush the stage,
tearing their hair out, ripping their clothes—
Excuse me while I kiss the sky...

The Morse Code of the open road,
dots and dashes in luminous yellow—
an SOS—
which soon turns into the unbroken
double line that leads to the end
of everything you know and fear
(not much just yet):
hug it and you may live,
cross it and you die.
On the AM radio crackling voices
rattle on about places
you'll never see or hear of again—
muffler shops, pizza joints, beauticians' schools—
in the cramped, smoke-shrouded cities
you're passing in the night.
Until you slow for a pileup in the opposite lane—
a burning van, a jackknifed tractor-trailer—
and cars lined up to rubberneck
as the cops and ambulances arrive
and a song comes on the radio
about reaching a place beyond heaven and hell.
A song you'll hear again, many times, over the years.

12

Setting out a tarot deck,
a Ouija board and planchette,
and a chip of marble from the amphitheater at Delphi,
we put red bulbs in the lamps
and pass around a hookah filled with crème de menthe,
seeking the possibility that the karma
in this shuttered room, at this instant,
will somehow be unblocked and clarified:
that the chains binding us
to the gate of iron,
the wooden post,
the immovable self—
all the things in this life intended to kill us off before our time—
are chains of water,
if only we could let them go,
let them flow...

13

Sleeping in a cold room on the Rue de Rennes,
counting the stars through the icy skylight,
steeping oolong tea and boiling fusilli on the wood stove.
Everything carefully accounted for:
wood: 40 francs a cord;
tea: 20 francs for 4 ounces;
fusilli: 30 francs a kilo.
The real heat,
under a purple quilt from the Arab quarter,
is provided by your body,
which unknown to us,
is already being eaten away by the cancer
that will kill you before the year is out.
Your funeral plot in Vevey: 2,000 francs.
In the room off this room where you work
you'll leave behind a set of lithographs:
Arctic landscapes in silver light.
I remember the day you began them.
Your blond hair flying by the river.
The children in pale blue robes begging for alms.
The plane trees blackening at dawn.
And those stars through the skylight:
the brightest of them no star at all,
but Venus, never flickering,
that forever after will rule my life.

You burn your haiku
about ships on fire written
last night at white heat

In a sleeping car from Paris to Marseilles
we never sleep
drinking a liqueur blue as the sky
from steel tumblers
while the stations of the night fly by
like bits of broken jewelry,
and you're chain-smoking the clove cigarettes
with the picture of the swami on the pack
who looks like the man we saw the police fish
from the Seine yesterday,
ocher-colored with mud for hair,
rotting leaves falling away from his body
as they eased him into a tossing motorboat....
Nearing Moulins, where the tracks narrow
coming out of the freight yards,
we douse our lamp
and draw the sheet to our chins
just as the northbound express thunders by,
leaving in its wake
the darkness of dawn to fill our mouths,
colder than water
and heavier.

We're on a mountain overlooking Spain that can only be climbed
    from France.
In one of those countries that is not really a country, called
    Andorra.
Stones white as skulls dot the stream flickering behind the trees.
The same stones from which this farmhouse was built long ago.
The wine in the cellar, from Morocco, is black in a black bottle,
on its label a cluster of stars on a circular vine—
like Ariadne's corona, glittering among the constellations.
In the fireplace we crisscross planks from the burned-down barn
while blown snow, fine as sand, glazes the windows.
When I cut the loaf of bread we brought from the village,
I find a gold coin, neither Spanish nor French,
on which a woman with outspread wings
and flying hair is perched on a moonlit peak.
A coin which the following evening in town purchases us
a sumptuous dinner and a choice room at the tiny hotel
where the proprietor says we may remain as long as we like,
so rare is that coin, minted in Andorra itself—
a country with no mint and no currency of its own.

17

The road to the hospital winds through a barren cornfield.
It's my friend's twenty-first birthday, the same month as my own.
He's in an oxygen tent, barely conscious.
A red bulb in the bedside lamp softens the room's hard edges.
Sitar music is playing on a tape recorder.
As I enter, the nurse is setting up his IV,
trying to find a clean vein among the track marks
he left on his arms like a road map:
the main roads red, the side roads blue,
the roads-under-construction dots and dashes....
The radiologist with a moon face tells me he has two months to
    live.
The surgeon with a hatchet face says it might be even less.
At the end of the corridor, the woman mopping with ammonia,
a charm bracelet jangling on her wrist,
whistles under her breath: a high-pitched tune
(from a Schumann fantasia) audible only to dogs.
What they didn't find in his blood, urine, saliva, or lymph fluid
turned up in his bone marrow.
"It's like a death warrant," the hematologist intones.
Once he set out to memorize the Prose Eddas.
Those Icelandic gods on thrones of broken rock
know that this life lasts no longer than the spark
thrown off when a hammer strikes an anvil.
Through the blue window that reflects the lights
of his vital signs dimming on a monitor
a snowstorm blows in from the prairie and frames
a pretty girl crossing the parking lot, tossing her hair.

18

All the maps in the world are burning from the outside in.
Consuming everyone, even those of us shivering
on the edges of obscurity,
the fear, deeper than marrow, frozen in our bones.
Here on the roof of a thirty-story building before dawn,
smoking blond hash in a Pyrex pipe—
smoke the color of the moon's aureole—
I unbutton your ankle-length tie-dyed dress
beneath which you're wearing nothing
but a black garter belt and white cowboy boots.
This is one of those moments
when the clouds open and we forget
everything we thought we knew.
The beehive lights of skyscrapers,
the jets filled with pilgrims,
the sirens of the ambulances speeding the dead across town,
the trains rumbling beneath the pavement:
it's all magnified into a single blinding point of light
that flickers in your eye
as your lips part
and you cry out—
the remaining hours of your life arcing by us like a cold rainbow—
and pull me closer whispering your own name.

19

A white sailboat on the black sea;
the clouds cresting, high in the sky, like waves;
the moonlight falling just so
on forests, lakes, and mountains,
on the hidden castle and the abandoned lighthouse:
none of it will survive the night.
And you and I,
we'll be gone too,
soon after stumbling on a back alley
from which a child whose shoes
are laced together around his neck
steps into the light of dawn
with a song on his lips
and a knife in his teeth.

20

Along the autobahn that bisects the river valley
enormous factories pour a second—darker—
sky beneath the one we haven't seen since crossing the Alps.
"There will be a lunar eclipse," the cashier at the truck stop
confides to us, "in fifty minutes."
When we pull over to view it,
moving vans, diesel trailers, and gasoline tankers
stream past us in a deafening wave.
And then motorcycles with blond women
in leather alert in the sidecars.
We see nothing of the moon, but we feel its tug
in the heavy air, sliding drops of sweat along
our brows and beading them on our temples.
Slowing the flow of blood into our hearts.
A thousand kilometers to the north,
beneath a snow-lined tree,
we're studying our map
when a troupe of Gypsies emerges
from the forest playing flutes and castanets.
A young woman with a face like clay,
lighting a cigarette, tells us we will never die
if we burn that map here and now. *Now!*
We burn it, and she blows a smoke ring
which later that night, or the next night—
long after she has disappeared—
encircles the moon.

21

In the lounge of the Athens airport
where Japanese terrorists recently machine-gunned the plate glass
   windows
a girl is writing a poem with her lipstick
on the front page of a newspaper.
The poem is in Spanish,
the newspaper is Dutch,
and the lipstick is the color of a blood-orange.
The girl, in a long white dress and a sailor cap,
sandals, silver bracelets, and a black ribbon tied around her neck—
my kind of girl—
lets me buy her a cup of chamomile tea
but won't tell me her nationality.
"I'm from an occupied country," she says,
"which therefore is no longer a country at all."
I try to guess:
Hungary, Latvia, Czechoslovakia, Northern Ireland...
"No no no," she shakes her head,
"and even if I showed you my passport you wouldn't know.
It's been taken off the map, blacked out, left to history.
You know.
The place where the ashes of things are so cold
you can't remember that they ever burned."

22

There is a white clock on the wall.
A black plant on the windowsill.
A black-and-white movie on the snow-filled
television screen in the Laundromat this snowy night.
In the movie, the woman in the black hat
and coat, a white rose in her lapel,
paces an icy parapet twirling an umbrella.
At midnight in the apartment upstairs
a man is preparing his supper:
an olive omelette with black bread and blackberry jam.
Smoke is swirling into the night,
and the naked girl on the coarse white sheets
is flicking a lighter that won't light,
a hand-rolled cigarette between her lips,
a black cat dreaming the dream in which time stops
lying across her ankles
with a tail regular as a metronome
but silent
into the dark dawn.

23

The rain crossing the tarred rooftops stops suddenly.
The wine I'm drinking is bright yellow,
centered with white lights.
The bread you're breaking is veined like marble,
gold and white.
A man comes to the door.
Then a woman.
We hear tambourines, a mandolin, a taut drum down the steep
    stairwell.
All night they accompany the dancers.
There is a doctor on the Bergenstrasse
who will sell us opium crystals.
His nurse wears a green dress and black stockings.
She is always on the telephone,
peering through the venetian blinds at the arcade
where old men in children's clothes line up
to shoot pellet guns at metal ducks.
This accounts for the truckload of stuffed animals at the corner.
Now it's afternoon again.
The water in the water pipes in this building has turned to blood.
The windows are barred with sunlight—stronger than steel.
Color me black.
White.
Gold.
And cover me.
I'm cold.

The doors undulate on hinges of water.
The ceiling is one with the sky.
A single chair, spotlit, centers the room
where the full moon floats inside a cello.
Here is a man who claims to correspond with Joseph Haydn in
    heaven.
Here is his page turner languid in a long black gown.
Clouds are pouring from her handbag, full of rain.
There is music—we can hear it—deep and steady,
but from far away,
through the park and the forest,
past the boats on the river
and the many places connected only by the river
before it pours into the sea.
All of us will leave this place hearing the music of the sea,
as if a shell has been pressed to our ears—
the one that was filled with our rushing blood
even before we were born.

Maya who weaves illusions
and casts the light from men's eyes—
the temptress of the *Dhammapada*—
turns down my bed in a suburb
of this factory town,
in the yellow house
with a caged canary in the foyer
and the shadow of a panther roaming the basement.
Maya who waits tables,
punches train tickets,
turns tricks,
who presses you to the floor
with her nipples brushing your lips
and her own lips parting slowly
on the empty vowel
that fills the mouths of those
with nothing to say, nothing to fear,
which strikes me—
thirsty at the crossroads
where a weather-stripped tree
offers the only shade—
to be one and the same.

26

The nightclub lies in a labyrinth of tunnels
beneath the rain-swept streets.
Beginning at midnight, the acts are:
a one-armed clown who plays the violin,
a stripper with three breasts,
a pair of talking dogs that converse in Chinese,
and—the finale—an androgynous couple
done up as mermaid and merman
who copulate underwater in a glass tank.
At the bar, under green lights, a line of men
in identical green suits stare into martini glasses
that widen every hour, like whirlpools.
The bartender's black glasses reflect everything
many times—like an insect's eye.
The waitresses are multiarmed-armed, like Shiva,
and some of them have wings.
And then there's the band:
bass, drums, piano, and clarinet,
to which the clown adds his violin
and one of the dogs the castanets
as they become a sextet
and play without interruption until dawn,
when the bouncer, blinking, with blood-stained knuckles,
coughs into his sleeve
and all the lights come up—
slowly, like the sun.

As the sun gilds the Arno and shades the stern faces
of the angels atop the cathedral,
two busses collide, toppling a statue of Machiavelli,
fire sweeps a school for the blind,
a nun finds an apple ripening on a pear tree.
At my hotel an old woman is crossing the lobby
in a shimmering dress
with a parrot on her shoulder
who is said to possess knowledge
of stars not yet born,
dreams not yet dreamed
crimes not yet committed.
After the hills darken and the torn clouds scatter,
the parrot ascends to a palm tree
in the mezzanine and begins squawking
names, dates, places—
his particular secret history of the living and the dead
that may never come to pass.

28

The German film is dubbed in English with Greek subtitles
and after six rounds of raki
my companion for the night,
who speaks only French,
proclaims it a masterpiece.
Her fishhook earrings are baited with flashes of moonlight.
Her lipstick sparkles like rain.
At 2 A.M. at a discothèque by the sea
she kicks off one shoe, then the other,
drops the straps of her gold dress,
and tosses her hair from shoulder to shoulder
while dancing with other men
and with me
and then, finally, alone, her back against the wall.
Later she will surprise me.
Not in the alley, cloudy with the scent of hibiscus,
where we stop to neck in a cone of light,
or in bed, kicking off the blue sheets,
but on my balcony, gazing at the warships
anchored on the horizon, when, huddled naked,
an unlit cigarette between her lips,
she addresses me for the first time in perfect English.
The girl in that film who drowned said love is the only crime.
Understand—I am no criminal.

A church filled with fiery flowers,
with widows in white and brides in black, milling.
At the midpoint of this broiling summer,
as waves of napalm crest in jungles
on the other side of the world
where every second someone is dying for nothing
while someone else is being sacrificed
in the name of something larger than himself,
I'm an island on an island
of two thousand living people
and five millennia of diaphanous souls
who have journeyed beyond the sun to become
(according to Hipparchus, himself born here)
stars, each of them, on the sphere that encloses
all things, including this girl dancing
along the seawall with bloodied feet,
trailing a fishnet delicate as lace,
the flame of her hair fanned by the wind
and her eyes bright as the candles
the mourners carry through the town at night,
every night,
down the same sequence of alleys
to the sea.

A single star burns above a black palm.
The moon's rays spray over the mountain peaks,
across the orchards and the tall grass,
onto the cresting waves beyond the cove.
We'll stay here for three nights
before I drive north
and you sail farther south—
as far as you can go.
We'll never meet again,
but for years I will glimpse your reflection in mirrors—
in hotel rooms, restaurants, trains—
always the same downcast eyes and baleful smile
and the words I can never quite decipher
forming on your lips:
something you wanted to tell me,
or something that I longed to hear?
More likely, as happened in that place
with the solitary palm and its shadow—
creeping across the sand to be erased by surf—
something that had nothing to do with me at all.

A man in a green coat is digging a hole beside a walnut tree.
A girl is swimming naked in a pond.
This cold white wine, from the bottle, goes down like fire,
clouding my vision.
Over France, over Spain, the skies are steely
and the fields are sunbaked.
Following the coastline at dawn,
I saw no fishing skiffs, no ocean liners,
not even a gull skimming the waves.
The last newspaper I bought, in Paris,
was filled with photographs of the war:
body bags on the deck of an aircraft carrier,
smoldering earth where a village once stood,
an entire jungle on fire.
We're lucky to be here, a hitchhiker observed
in a Texas drawl,
slapping the dust from his jacket
beneath the shadow of a crooked tree.
I agreed with him, and now I'm wondering
what the man in the green coat will bury in that hole;
wondering, too, about the luck of another man,
out of sight until that moment,
who rises languidly with grass-stained pants
to hold a towel for the girl emerging
from the pond, shaking out her hair.

My dying landlady's beautiful daughter Bellona—
namesake of the Roman goddess of war—
strolls the beaches pocketing star-speckled shells.
When I kiss her in the doorway one night
to the clattering of cicadas
and the plaintive crescendos of the clown
singing on her mother's phonograph,
she lays my hand on her breast
and brushes my ear with a whisper
that will linger in my memory
long afterward, like the wind at this moment
which is blowing in off the sea,
dusting the cypresses and the long streets,
and Bellona's parted lips, with salt.

33

I'm carrying a knapsack filled with books
up the stairs of the rooming house in Barcelona,
my boots wet from the sea,
my fingers stained by the harsh cigarettes
I'm smoking all day and half the night
when a woman on the topmost landing,
her features twisted up,
lipstick smeared across her cheek,
rushes from one door to another brandishing a knife.
No sound ensues, no scream or cry—nothing.
Just dust floating in a beam of the setting sun.
And from the street the Gypsy wearing a top hat
who introduces himself as Pan
is still playing his one tune on a wooden flute.
It's not in one of those books on my back
that I'm discovering the fact
there are spaces around every human being
which can never—should never—
be filled by anyone or anything.
Discovering, too, that the bright blur
which occasionally occupies some corner of my sleep
or catches my eye from a speeding train
may be my own soul escaping me,
as it must, many times in this life,
each time slipping a little farther away.

On the southern coast of Crete
where even the shadows of the palms smolder
and tumblers of raki waft smoke
and steam pours from bursting melons,
naked girls are lolling, burnt-orange, in the boiling surf.
They live in the black caves along the beach,
and for a week I'm one of their guests,
drinking wine mixed with honey,
making love between handwoven blankets,
gazing cross-legged at the thin line
that is Africa shimmering on the horizon.
Some Americans in loincloths have founded
a school of Pythagoras in a hut beneath the cliffs.
They eat only figs, olives, and barley cakes
and at nightfall play lutes and timbrels
and watch stars across the galaxy conjoin into circles
which mesh like the gears of a clock,
measuring—to the last second—every man's life.

35

All afternoon the workmen are pouring cement,
reinforcing the church's foundation
before receiving communion from the priest.
A rooster parades the peaked roof,
circling the cross hammered out of sunlight.
Songbirds fill the lime trees.
The saints in the stained glass windows stare out to sea.
Downing black coffee, smoking oval cigarettes,
I sit awash in fast shadows.
Open before me is the pocket edition of the *Inferno*
I bought in Florence months ago;
all around me are tourist girls—
Swedish, French, Japanese—
sunburnt and scantily dressed,
who are boarding a bus
for Aphrodite's temple at Lindos.
A tourist myself, passport in hand,
tracing my finger over the map
at the end of Canto XXXIV—
the one that charts the way to purgatory—
I can only hope the border guards there,
forever warming their hands over an unlit stove,
will wave me through.

Cactus from which a scrap of clothing—
sky-blue—
flaps in the hot wind.
Mountains jagged as flames encircling a lunar landscape.
A junked car stripped to its chassis.
Between the two dried-out riverbeds
someone has propped three dead men around a fire
where black beans, bacon, and garlic
are simmering in a rusted pot
and a radio with failing batteries is tuned
to a station that plays the same song
all night: a grief-stricken woman
soaring the higher octaves,
anchored by a bass line steady as a pulse
until—when we least expect it—
her voice breaks.
On what mission were these men embarked
when Death overtook them?
And you, where will you be,
and with whom,
and with what darkness yawning in your heart,
when she overtakes you?

37

In this seaside hotel on the Costa Brava
where the cacti glow like molten iron
I drift in and out of the same dream
every night for a week:
I'm on an ocean liner cutting through
a great harbor lined with towers.
Stars streak behind the purple clouds.
Green flames dance from the smokestacks.
Lightning bolts light up the bridges.
The city is Manhattan.
I'm coming home with an empty suitcase
and no one to meet me.
At dawn the chambermaid,
singing in Catalan,
enters my room with a tray
of boiled eggs, bitter coffee, and figs.
She shaves me before the tarnished mirror,
over the triangular sink,
with a straight-edge razor.
She buttons up my collarless shirt.
Laces my high black boots.
Presses her breasts against my chest.
On the windowsill a turtledove sings.
Sunlight floods the plain.
If I close my eyes,
I can hear the clatter of faraway streets,
can feel them humming beneath the soles of my feet.

Today while snow slants into Manhattan,
the black and white flakes
like sparks off a flint,
two men step onto the moon.
Their footprints will remain in the deep dust
long after the last man has walked the earth.
While icicles bar the window
and snakes hiss in the radiators,
I remain in your bed all day, jet-lagged,
a cashmere blanket pulled to my chin
until you return from work,
unzip your dress,
unfasten your bra,
peel off your stockings
and slide in beside me with the cold
scent of the wind in your hair.
While the astronauts who left Florida
three days ago wander the airless valley
of Taurus-Littrow on the moon's equator,
my mouth finds yours,
your breath fills my lungs,
the blue of your eyes spills over like water.
From the earth, the moon glows white;
from the moon, the earth is starkly lit;
but at 3 A.M. when you cross the room naked,
it's your body that shines so bright.

The books are piled high in the corners:
Blake, Céline, Bulgakov, Kleist,
Li Po and Jarry,
Suetonius and Procopius,
and the complete works of Fyodor Mikhailovich Dostoevski.
The ashtrays are overflowing.
A candle stuck in an empty vodka bottle is burning at noon.
A photograph of Wild Bill Hickok has been blown up, wall-size.
Let It Bleed is playing on the phonograph
with four LPs stacked above it.
In the soup pot on the stove carrots and potatoes
are tumbling in boiling water.
The telephone is ringing in another room.
The doorbell is ringing in another life.
Who will come through that door,
across time and space,
defying laws of life and death,
to deliver a message.
Something like: *You think you're here, but you're not here.*
Or: *Years from now you'll try to imagine*
this instant and yourself so lost in it.
Or maybe yourself just oblivious:
to the express trains racing through the night
with their upright passengers masquerading as the dead;
to the sun's myriad satellites reflecting its rays;
to the snatch of dialogue, from a dream, which someone scrawled
on the bathroom mirror with purple lipstick.
Yes, who was it who did that?

I'm in a bar alone
not drinking
staring at a television perched
among the shelves of bottles and stuffed birds
herons and kingfishers
following the clusters of bombs spinning down
into a forest where women and children
huddle beneath the ticking bamboo counting
the seconds left to them in a world
where the moon is blackened
and the stars streaking earthward trail gasoline
vapors that ignite the grass hillsides
the thatch houses along the river
the river itself
flowing like lava into the village
which can only be reached by the wooden bridge
over the waterfall near the temple
where incense burns at a stone altar
and all those who will soon be ashes
bow their heads and close their eyes
and a solitary man reading his own palm
tries to distinguish between the living and the dead
as they edge along the cold line
that cuts the sky in two
twenty miles north of Quang Tri
a million light-years from anywhere

On the round water bed at the center of the room
a girl in a silver bikini and black goggles is basking
under a sunlamp on a mandala bedspread.
It's the last room in a railroad flat,
and at the other end of the crowded hallway
dense with smoke and incense
someone is picking out a Scarlatti sonata on an electric piano.
The girl's hair is bleached platinum.
Her lipstick is purple.
She's deeply tanned.
Some people in a circle are tossing coins
and deciphering the hexagrams of the *I Ching.*
Beyond the blackout drapes over the barred windows
enormous animals are roaming the streets,
engorged with the shadows of their prey.
Their heavy breathing makes me sweat
at the small round table
where I'm composing a chain poem
with two other poets and a blind woman
who has memorized the *Nibelungenlied.*
My contribution to the chain poem:
Radio waves are like ocean waves, concentrically flowing.
My contribution to the evening:
calculating how I will end up on the water bed
when everyone else is gone and the sunlamp is extinguished,
taking in that girl's tropical secrets,
her traveler's tales from faraway lands.

Ice drips from the thorns in the roof garden.
Tinfoil birds perch on bare branches.
The weathervane is frozen,
the thermometer has cracked.
At a window three stories down
two women are singing "Silent Night,"
harmonizing as if they are all alone in the world.
In the otherwise darkened building
the light from that window is flowing
out into the night,
like the beam of a ship at sea.
It is 4 A.M.,
two weeks before Christmas.
Up and down the black street
no one is approaching this building
and no one is leaving it.
Under snowdrifts there are parked cars,
burrowing mice, bums in sleeping bags.
Clouds are sliding across the graphite sky.
You're following them, wide-eyed,
as bells start ringing
where the stars would be
if there were stars.

43

Trucks are salting the streets.
The airports have closed.
In this long empty room the shadow
of a lemon tree flutters on the wall.
The last record played hours ago,
but the stereo's lights,
like rubies and emeralds,
continue to flicker.
The blanket on the bed is paper-thin,
the pillow is like stone.
I was dreaming of myself
in such a bed,
drawing a map that encompassed
all the cities I just passed through—
Paris Trieste Athens Ravenna—
except that it resembled a map
of the Amazonian jungle,
vast forests and countless tributaries
off a serpentine river.
Until I wake up, I feel certain
this map could have guided me around Europe,
or anywhere else I chose to go.
Meanwhile, through the frozen window,
an ocean liner, white as an iceberg,
is sailing down the Hudson
for the open sea.

From my corner table beneath a blue light
the palms are swaying,
the drummer's steel brushes slide
across his ride cymbal like an ocean wave.
A woman wearing a black dress
imprinted with white roses
refills her wineglass,
closes her eyes, and finds herself
transported to a velodrome
banked like the rings of Saturn.
Closing my eyes, I travel more modestly,
to the recent memory of Saint Nicholas
eyeing me severely from the wall panel
of a chapel on the island of Poros,
where the streets are whitewashed daily.
Here on Manhattan Island it takes a blizzard
to whitewash the streets,
and the gods who reveal themselves to us
are famously pitiless, cold, and rife with knowledge.
Walled in by bricks of ice,
illuminated by a guttering candle,
you (or someone impersonating you)
begin explaining the mechanics of salvation
before preceding me into the snow,
the wind that rattles our bones like sticks,
the night like a vast tide that carries all things away.

Tomorrow, the New Year, the world begins anew.
Or so they say.
Some will depart this place.
Others will remain.
A few will count themselves lucky.
Many will be unlucky.
Just before midnight, I drift away
from my third party in as many hours
and find myself in a darkened room
overlooking the park, the swaying treetops
laden with snow beneath a rising moon.
It was once thought the souls
of the dead resided on the moon,
in glass buildings like this one,
and, for diversion, gazed to earth,
at the wars, famines, and migrations,
the floods and fires that destroyed whole cities.
The Apollo astronauts who just walked on the moon
will be the last men to do so in this century.
When one of them visited Nepal soon afterward,
children lined the mountain roads with candles
and bowed to him as they would to a god.
Tonight if there are gods looking down at us,
at our own follies and disasters,
will they continue merely to order our fates
(even as we resolve to change them),
or will they embrace us at last
in all their splendor, and set us free?